AF287280

Diana Mistera

Before the dawn ...

...after the dusk

"Before the dawn, after the dusk", is a poetry book of Diana Mistera. It is a collection of poems, ranging from 2011 to 2019.

Kustantaja: BoD – Books on Demand, Helsinki, Suomi

Valmistaja: BoD – Books on Demand, Norderstedt, Saksa

ISBN: 9 789528 024675

The poet's hand writes the theme with care
when the dawn still hides the fading night.
Love is what she finds,
although a shadow just shape shifted into a wolf.

Prologue

Diana Mistera brings us an intimate poetry collection about the encounter with love in the paradoxical situation of being in a different reality. The separation can be symbolized by a mirror, a dream or death.

The gothic background of the author, already seen in two of her books from the series Orpheus, comes back transformed in a sea of verses, poems that seem to be waves coming from a deep and unknown place. This sea enfolds the poetic persona until it gives her the shape of someone who can float and survive.

The darkness and the gentle light go together, as do the pain and the pleasure. Lost love is an invisible lifebelt, which will be released from its task when she comes ashore and is aware of a new reality.

The poems take us beyond the understanding of time and dreaming.

It is possible to swim in a free verse that suddenly brings in a stanza of oxygen and rhymes. They make us wonder about the differences between memories and dreams.

The poems in "Between the darkness and the dusk" are

reinforced with many references to Greek mythology, and to Latin and Italian languages, which point out the Mediterranean origin of Mistera.

The same fresh breeze can be felt in the construction of some verses.

Music has been a deep source of inspiration for the poet. She even writes a note for the reader under one of the poems, which is unforeseen and kind.

Zoila Forss

III AWARENESS

MY THANX TO   77

Diana Mistera

Before the dawn....

...After the dusk

2020

BEFORE THE DAWN, AFTER THE DUSK

And it is precisely the dawn with her touch, that make the shadows lose their consistency, and the dusk that wriggled my dreams.

I cross the limbo with my usual uncertainty, right there, on the borderline between the reality and the dream, I become unsecure even of my senses, doubting the very existence of the world in which I am guest in this certain time range, unsure I am wondering if the night journey has not been nothing more than a glimpse of a parallel reality tied to my soul.

I feel you

the boundary between life and death is as thin as the needle that carve your skin.

I'm afraid that Charon endue by a sudden mercy, granted a last visit before carrying you in Hades.

I cannot breathe

I feel suffocated

I cannot move or even get up.

I wait the awaking of the sun to challenge those loads that have collapsed on me, remove those stones that are immobilizing me.

I greedily drink the light, grab my memories, before they are gone,

finally free from the agony of a dream.

Welcome sun, welcome gentle light, release me from those horrible shadows that smell like sulphur.

I wish to be there while you are still asleep, whispering how much I love you, in one of your dreams. Would be enough to give you the strength you need, to fight against your fiends.

Our souls are bounded by the same fate but shifting traces in an undisclosed reality.

HAUNTING YOU

I have always been a traveller

blessed with the gift of the seer

looking for certainty all the time

too unsure of everything.

In the past year I wondered without you.

Trying to find a meaning of this life, this thing...

wondering if what I saw and feel,

was real, or just a chimera,

I couldn't neither touch you, the way I needed and need.

Wondering about my choices.

I am still a wanderer.

It had hurt wait and see nothing was happening.

It had left me hopeless believe,

it was just me and my wishful thinking

to miss heavily what we had

somewhere else around the universe

scared to have lost it all here.

Those nights have been cold

my eyes were blind

but now I know, you never left my side

silently waiting for me to feel you again.

I did, I do; but blindness is confusing, you know...

I know you could give me only that

it wasn't and it isn't enough

you know this too now.

Maybe you neither knew what you where doing

and why you always find yourself there, with me,

a perfect stranger probably, but so familiar, so glasslike

Was it a trick of our mind?

Too good to be true?

No, I assure you, it was real

and you probably have get it before me.

It is scary, isn't it?

Well I read you...

Come near now, I am waiting you to hold me,feel me.

We are trapped this carcass full of limits

but I want you to know, I would surely stay

"When the time is right" you say.

PROMISE

I want to believe that is not my obsession

which flows where only desires dare.

My brain is burning

my defences are down

and I feel vulnerable

afraid that everything will vanished

in the very moment I will say the words.

I cannot bare anymore the pain

I don't know what to do

confusion has put its roots in me

questioning everything that I have believed in.

The dreams once were my shelter

now they are delusions in disguised

filling me with scares and scars

leading me astray.

Don't give up on me

my heart is heavy

but you'll find my love there for sure

make me believe again

and I will love you endlessly.

SCOREKEEPER

From the very beginning
we were like dancing magnets
of fragmented molecules
which were an entirety once.
We collide in each other's life
and couldn't stop what
was rising from within.
Once we were silver lining scars
and we fed our desire
with tongues of fire
Now we crackle and torn
burning every time a bit more.

THE WATCHER

I am The Watcher
Coursed, after The Great Fall.
I guard you while you sleep
I protect you from the demons in your dreams
feeling a daemon myself
with my wings in chains.
In the silence I whisper to you
I look at the years passing on your skin
while the eternity awaits
slowly your light is fading away.
Fly with me, fall with me
Will you die for me?
The fear which is causing your soul to freeze
it is indeed what make your darkest dreams
A rain of roses crimson fire
unchaste desire unleashed
the despair become my hail
Love, my decay.

FACELESS

Digging in all the blue days

observing

my reflection going by in a mirror.

We all have our part in this play

building lies after lies

Changing masks after masks

looking for the character that is a better fit

Filling this artificial happiness

that built the fable

just

to make the poison of life less bitter

and death tread slower.

Drunk on my tears

words came alive while my screen blurred

and in that very moment

I decided to throw away all my masks,

and here I am

faceless

trapped in this eternal dream of you.

TIME

Time to cast aside all the demons

that have been deceiving my heart in the past.

Time to chase the shadows

in a path without traces.

Time to jump in the unknown

leaving this sense of alienation

which turned a victory into a misery.

Time to foresee the lines

written on a deserted road.

Time

a shadow hunted by poets

and the oldest illusion

of a bleeding heart.

CONFINED

I sleep between the gates of time
although my world
has turned to ashes,
I'm still its guardian.

You have dreamt of me sometimes
I was your best friend
the steadfast one
when you came around.

I am the last of my kin
caressing you with my kisses
disappearing in the haze
when you opened your eyes
diving the frozen scenes
I got what you meant
although I am confined.

EVERMORE

Forever is a word

that means more than people think

so deep the meaning

that embraces eternity

You say it once

close your eyes in the night

call my name and I will be right by your side

lighting a candle calling your name

certain that

you are somehow coming.

THE MIRROR

The mirror was there
and as I approached, it sucked me.
I whirled like in a black hole
leaving behind me only pale reflections.
Willing prey of this untamed dream
longing for more to achieve.
Right there you were
the tainted dreamer
you called me knowing
I was the eternal seeker.
The darkness faded
everything changed with a slight movement of my face
leaving me wondering
if I was trapped in your same,
complex structure,
or, was I meant to be,
only the silent watcher?

FIRE AND ICE

My heart burned
and in a scream
was hidden your name,
no one heard it, but you.
The flames crafted an image,
frozen in time.
Since the very moment in which
the fire stigmatized their fate
two souls entwined
became eternally confined.

SLEEPLESS NIGHT

Another sleepless night staring at the starless sky
I am hidden behind the red curtains
and, even the rhythm of my heartbeat
is making to much noise.
Beat my heart and bleed
there are no winners tonight
in this battlefield
you, with all your riddles
and question marks
are leading the assault squad
ignoring
I am already on my knees
with the white flag.

NEMESIS

Did you ever felt love in the eclipse of the sun?
Everything is still
The present is floating in the nothingness
and the future is on stand.
Silence, and the cold caress of the breeze
run on the skin.
The soul recall its nemesis
for a moment even the time has no barriers.
Ghost are chasing their preys
you know
shadows can't stand companions
but they seek with bittersweet desire
a moment that went lost.
I live for the night
just to find you there
drifting roles
we have been over there for too long
longing for the comfort of each others arms
give me a reason why, we are still on the run.

Struggle

BOULEVARD OF BROKEN DREAMS

Boulevard of Broken Dreams

is the street you think to walk alone

until you notice to be surrounded by clones

disguised as dim shadows, shapeless.

Is there the line, to catch the last ticket

to the next stop: Self Pity.

Didn't you know is free

for those who deserve the visit?

Don't stumble on those broken bricks

the one behind, is ready to run over you.

You feel heavier

every step you take, slower

while all your chances pass you by

heavier, slower,

every mistake you made, now you carry

heavier, slower, frozen

your soul is cracking

on the Boulevard of Broken Dreams.

WALLS

In this cold empty space

the walls are coming closer

I am building them again with all my fears

brick after brick

and I want to run, run away

and leave them behind

but wherever I turn I see other walls

and I don't have anymore the power to tear them down

How I end up here again?

I travelled through thousands lives

keeping searching, knowing

I will find you, each time on my path

loosing the gap on dreams and words along the way

Now on my knees

in front of this wall

I feel the heaviness of every choice we've made

and I just want you to hold me

assuring me you are behind it

to not give in but,

the sadness is killing me using my fears as weapon.

NOVEMBER SKY

I'm drifting through time
I 've wasted my powers for too long
I see the dimmed and lonely look
the mirror's reflect, not of myself.
I surrender the voices
gathering on the wind
some talk, other chant,
some howl, other breath into my body
and yesterdays become the ways of tomorrow.
Why you stare at me saying bleed well ?
Help me rise instead.
I can't ever keep from falling apart at the seams
And you're taking my heart piece after piece,
leaving my soul agonized, demanding for yours.
A radio tune, I swear I've heard before.
I'm lost in a snow filled sky
stranger, in a strange land
with dreams as companions
while slowly, I come undone.

MY NAME IS NOBODY

Welcome invisible

give your farewell

to the platform of the fame.

Welcome to the world of nothingness

where the humming machines

have more voice than yours.

Welcome to those

that wanted to listen

but they born deaf.

Welcome to those that wanted to see

but they born blind.

Welcome to all those phantoms

that creeping and cry

but are not able to fly.

Welcome to all the scum

that the world is giving you for sale

nobody is interested on your tale.

I welcome you all

with the smile on my face.

My name is Nobody.

CAST AWAY

There are doors

that can't be closed at night

and balances

that can't be broken at daylight

and there is

the stillness of some days

an heavy load to carry

even if I was a giant.

You are there, you always have been there

your shadow follows

and in silence you wait.

I was sure I did let you go

I thought

you have set me free

and by my will

I followed you once again.

There is not a victory or a defeat

Love is, what make the heart bleed.

You are playing around once again

while I am torn between halos and demons
lost in words with cryptic meanings.
If only I could dare but...
I turn my eyes and walk away,
crying in the cold winter rain
singing in silence my ode to the pain.

MY FALLEN

Frozen in that moment
seems my time stood still
but, everything was falling apart
and it fell, where everything begins.
Life and death combine
in the one and only ring, eternally.
The sun rises every morning
seems that nothing had changed
but its light is slipping away from me.
I look at to the moon
there, is the little girl that once I was
and you are still holding my hand.
The night becomes
the only time that the sorrow goes away
the Dark embrace me silently
the stars become my tears
I don't have to explain, why I feel lost
He never asks questions but,
who are those faceless strangers around me?

THE LAST RUN

The dreams are going wild

with the sound of burning shame

I heard your soul cry

when the hunger grew high

dive dark knight

through endless empires

ride the moonlight

run for your last bite

before the night dies.

FALL

Around the universe
our roles are switched
and I am wondering
if you are counting the dead leaves.
Soft rain is falling
and in front of me a yellow carpet
has been unrolled by the Fall
but it leads to nowhere
beside a tombstone
I look at the trees
they are waiting to freeze.
The silence is biting
leaving only space
for a leaf that is fading.
Ghosts are whispering,
why Is nobody coming
A lonesome bird is guarding
a tombstone no longer remembered.

THERE ARE MANY WAYS TO DIE

Once one told me
there are many ways to die
you should have warned me
when I saw you the first time.
Memories floated
long way behind.
I have crossed centuries
I had pass the line.
A strange confusion
faked those illusions
make me forget all the disillusions.
There are many ways to die
love, was mine.
Nights without lights
lights with no soul
a heart made of stone
went lost on the road
constantly filling it
with too many gravestones.

In front of me died the agony.

Behind the tore veil was you

whom arise from the ashes

giving me, one more reason to believe

there always be light

at the end of the darkness.

The broken mirror

doesn't give me anymore, the beauty of a lie

I see instead

how the truth crackles with its many faces.

DREAM

Your soul was attached at you with every single cell
and at the universe with every single atom.
You were singing or maybe screaming
the invisible pain that you are carrying
It was a bright light that it diffused
but it has a worried sight on you
like one of those celestial beings
that try to talk unheard.
You look strong as much as weak
and as fast as the light moved
I realized I was looking a picture.
An eternal memory frozen
of an unspeakable anguish
whispered only at the moon.

FAREWELL

I carry all your secrets under my skin
and seal everything with this my last kiss.
The air around me still feels like a cage
and I feel I cannot breathe
my heart beats so fast that echoed in my ears
it was just yesterday I told you my Farewell.
Now I feel empty and confuse
but I cannot cry, and I don't know why.
Maybe because although was a closure
it was yet again beautiful
like the first time when everything started.
How a farewell can feel beautiful?
Maybe because it wasn't a farewell after all.
I love you enough to let you go
but you cannot actually walk away from someone
if your soul had decided to stay
so I run away before you know
wearing my smile as better as I could
while deep inside I was at war with my feelings.

I let you at your fate
and break myself on the way
you gave me up to play safe
leaving me on my own
hanging on a hope.
Angels lie to keep control
but I am not an angel after all
and if you still care
don't ever let me know.

THERE IS NEVER AN END

Is pointless to try to find excuses

and lock away all memories

fooling myself that all those open scars

finally will stop bleeding

all the questions

eventually will get the right answers

and close this circle

which is still full of crackles.

The fire has sealed my soul to yours

and it burns

every time our universes collide

giving me an illusion

that I still believe to be real.

The waiting became agony

and the hope is killing me every time

I keep it high

but nothing goes the way I wanted to go.

And you are moving far away

in those dreams that once were happy and vivid

and now

I look at you unable to reach you

unable to hold you

The fire will always burn

and the rain will be always wet

I cannot ignore anymore the pain

but I can't let you go either

becoming myself

my own executioner.

BLOODLUST

Born in the silence
buried in the sands of time
there is a hidden flame;
yet must to be seen the fire within.
The sweet taste of your scarlet blood
the bittersweet of this ancient power
Give it to me, give in,
for my touch
for my taste for my lust.
Come out, come out, wherever you are
my bloodlust is craving for you
will you be forever mine?
Never stop craving
when you will be reaching for the wisdom
of those that have failed to become gods.

SUMMER SOLSTICE

The summer has started
with her nights without darkness
the heartache of the starless sky
where a wish is impossible
but the moon will be there near the sun at midnight
finally together at least for a few months.
Everything is as quiet as death
in this ghost city
where even the ghosts decided to run away.
The screams of the seagulls remind me
that something is alive
and I am not only a silhouette
is trying to escape
from black and white silent movie
The last beer can, reached the others
that are dead too.
A lonesome dreamer
with rotten dreams.

THE LAST CRUISE

Fading from the light
the darkness surrounded me
lost and lonely
with my soul was imprisoned
in what this body contained
looking at the empty shrine in vain.
Death surrounded me
with hundreds of souls
coming back from that journey.
Their final stop was
the boat with Charon at its wheel:
the last cruise began
Tears of loss, tears of pain,
the silent scream, the final hail.

DAMOCLES' SWORD

Thousands of thoughts poison your heart
feeding your fears
and you feel
the sword of Damocles hanging on you.
Every time it is coming closer
you wonder when it will hit
you feel already the cold blade slowly sever
there is no way out, nor back neither forward
everything is still, suspended.
You close your heart and soul
freezing everything that try to pass through
is the survival instinct
but don't you see that you are freezing yourself too?
Would you see the light again?
Would you feel the warmth again?
Don't let your heart die lonely and alone.
We are made from the same matter of the stars
let your flames shine bright
just feel the bliss of the universe.

Stand up now brave knight

cut the chains which keep you imprisoned,

you no longer need them

you have been through this before

let the sword be the tool for your victory

not the cause of your defeat.

FADING

I hear a distant voice
and I am falling apart
martyr of a decadence
that I no longer share
I let it burn to ashes.
Your eyes are begging
while the silence is screaming
and the soul fading
in a desperate no more.

DAMAGE

And again I fell in your trap
twisted angel
with the fire of a demon in your eyes
and an aware smile.
My wounds are wide open again.
Bleed my love bleed, you hiss
licked them until everything feel like nothing.
I know I need my scars
because when I play with you
I will be always without an armour.
I have been hidden in so many realities
and still you always have found me Mr. Pain
you always humbling waiting at the end of the line
so, better be your friend
instead have you as my enemy.

ASHES WITH MEMORIES

Forgetting is in vain

memories will be not washed away by the rain

or buried by the sand of time.

Counting the ciphers of tears I've spread

is hard to know

that each one

is a dream I left behind or forget.

I've burned to ashes and reborn thousands of times

the fire marked my soul

and my heart ablaze

with the only letter I never regret to send.

We are what we are

we can't be otherwise

our soul in entwined

but our worlds set us apart.

Awareness

ARE WE STRANGERS AT ALL?

As you whisper my name
I go in those prohibited places of my soul
feeling sometimes guilty
because the first time we met
I really couldn't stand you.
Now in my dreams you come
not anymore an unpleasant presence
you feed that doubt
and memories gathering around
You tell me stories
and every time I dream about you
I feel...I feel...I love.
You. Us.

SIN

The ancient serpent sealed the original sin

willing prey we have been

in the name of the sweetest dream.

Demonised by divine insights

blinded we believed

the everlasting love.

In eternal isolation

we perpetually seek

for each other's eyes

knowing that eternity

will not make us fall apart

but lost, in the circles of the merciless time.

I LOVE YOU

I light a candle
when the night is still young.
A silhouette appear
it has your shape
a familiar stranger without a name.
My heart knew you,
I can tell
because of the old ache
that pierced my soul with regrets
empty spaces between the words
"I will be forever yours".
I see your beautiful face in the mirror
and seal my fate with a kiss.
I was born free
craving those chains
and lost in a distant dream
I left everything begin.

ADDICTED

The world is standing still
I pray for the night to come
to reach you
and take you away with me
to fulfil my darkest dreams.
I am not an angel
and if I was once
now I've learned to fly
on broken wings.
Longing for you
I leap into the mirror
and on the other side
there is light no more.
Diving into the spotless night
I'm leaving all my memories behind.

OMEN

You walk away from the pain

you left behind

but without me

you lose your way.

Come, come to me

take my hand and believe.

No time to think

no time to keep

you can't pretend

That I don't exist.

Distances are what

make souls ramble

and hearts humble.

I am in your blood

I am under your skin

We walk along

through those parallel worlds

You are the one

I have been searching for so long

my sweetest poison, my eternal temptation.

CYPHER

I am searching answers in the clouds
many of them seemed to shape your face.
You lead me to a point
where everything is shifting and myself with it
everything is redesigned,
rewritten in ciphers that I am unable to decrypt.

In your eyes I see the mysteries of the Universe
they brought light to my life
and I love to get lost in them
although I never understand them.
Encryption decrypted
Ready to fly away, you spread my mind to play.
I see the secrets between the lines
pick them as they are rare flowers
that are growing only in the Savage Garden.

You're doing wondrous things to my soul.
Do them one more time,

Do to me what you want

I cannot get enough and

I'm thirsty for more until...

the cracking of the reality

ground me back in the uncertainties

back to that cipher that I cannot decrypt.

GAMER

The sun is shining warmly

everybody is laughing

on the shore of the lake

I see my pattern and smile as well,

just one direction in my thoughts.

I was the runner and now I am on the run

Feeling I am going nowhere

but still running.

Love could be magic

and sometimes start as a pinball game.

You are the plunger

and like a crazy ball I strike on the playfield

hitting every corner and bumper.

Skilled players know how to manipulate the game

in order to direct the ball towards a certain path.

Now,

I hope you know how to keep the game going

because I don't want to end as a game over.

Patience is not one of my virtues

and you are in my mind

no matter where I go or stay

So,

I dream my time away

we are together

wishful thinking, I guess

but now I feel the warm on me.

Strike, hit and tilt

you won this game long ago.

Did you know?

LOVE, PREJUDICE AND PRIDE

Is true, we were meant to find each others

and this took me by surprise,

and how unfair were the eyes,

when they laid thy sight into each others,

and unfair became then the fate.

As I stepped backward

I realized what I couldn't ignored

but it was so frightened.

So, I condemned myself

to stay in the shadow

always following,

always there for you,

waiting you to find me again

now that I am aware

that the beauty was not what divided

but the fear, the prejudice and the pride.

FIRST DAY OF THE YEAR...

As I wake in this silence

with the remains

of what has captured my heart

I walk by

and smile at the past;

my life is lying there

splitting into million pages already written

and there is no need

to remember all the ways

because they come once again

to restart from the beginning

knowing that

we will never be an empty page

torn apart.

∞ INFINITY ∞

Words disappear

leaving behind only echoes.

The lights went out

and the silence took its heavy place

in the front row

full of unspoken words

and, a dream was suddenly gone.

It was winter that led me to the pain

and

it was the spring that washed it away

with soft rain.

In the summer I was reborn with a new flame

but everything was leading to you,

once again.

COME BACK

Come back my fallen star

because every dawn you get more lost

Bind me with your grace

enchant me

show me your brightness

stop getting lost in the emptiness

Come back my little sun

when the winter is gone

the snow too comes undone.

Come back my darling one

come back to me my love.

CRIMSON IS THE POISON

Lost in the darkness

searching for the red line

knowing to find you there

waiting.

The moon coldly follows my every step.

The heart starts beating faster

exploding in my chest

bleeding out the words

you'll never hear

counting every tear

disguising the fear

counting the drops

of the scarlet poison within

preparing myself

for the last dream

ready to be entwined in eternity.

DREAMS ARE THE FALLEN ANGELS' WINGS

I dashed

off on a long journey

and exhausted I fell

thinking all my dreams had died.

Suddenly I was lifted up.

When I couldn't even crawl

your soft touch became stronger

 and your voice whispered

"never give up on your dreams

they are your wings

spread them wide

against the fear,

you never know when illusions become real. "

SOUL AND TEARDROPS

Soul, please take me

where joy and happiness will last.

Fate, breathe your last breath

where the heart will finally rest.

Take me away from the misery

of a memory I can't recall.

Teardrops falling

lightened by the moonlight

away from others sight

burning my soul from inside

in a moment frozen in the time:

face to face with your eyes in mine.

BELOVED EMPTINESS

Looking out of the window

while it's raining

counting every heartache

in each drop of rain

while my tears

still keep falling on the floor.

My heart is gasping

at the memory of your lovely smile

that used to be, only mine.

I am crumbling

out of the shadows

only to run back in there.

This emptiness I hoped would be gone

but its pain is keeping this love forever alive.

I don't know what I am feeling

Is it the cold feel of the grave?

Or is it only the edge of the black hole

that I am running straight into

knowing that

I always find you at the end of the tunnel.

THE OTHER SIDE OF THE MOON

Sometimes it seems

that the dark will last forever

you wake up

and all in a sudden your sky is without stars

and you feel like sinking

wonder if, will you ever touch the ground.

Your dreams are frozen

up there, on the moon

they say all the lost things end up there

on the other side of the moon

and staring at her light

think

everything will pass.

When you feel your heart is like a haunted place

every beat is a venomous bite

remember

also those who are afraid to die

they will die someday

so the nightmares

the emptiness and the sense of void

that sensible souls always feel.

You are beautiful

and you are strong

keep your fire alive

and ride the dark

with that flame in your heart.

*Note from the poet: I was listening the song "Moongirl " of Alphaville", when I felt the need to make a quotation of some of its beautiful words. Thanks for the inspiration.

INTERCOURSE

I penetrate your soul

bleeding through your dreams

soothe your wounds

shattering your broken wings

riding your soul until

you'll screaming lust

gasping in the emptiness

kissing the void left

before disappearing

in the mist of a dream unfinished.

LET MY HEART BURNS

And here I am

holding my breath and tears

feeling my heart bleeding.

Let me fall

and when I am crumbling

show me to whom I am holding.

There, where we start

you took my heart

and let me then fall apart.

Let the night fall

let the dawn born

let my heart burn

let your soul return

to me FOREVERMORE.

MY THANKS TO:

First of all I want to thank Zoila Forss, for the prologue and for the precious comments during the editing of this poetry book.

A special thanks goes to Teresa Bonaccorsi who has making the graphic inside the book, and Paolo Silvestri for the picture of the cover, which is one of my favourite spot in my beloved town Torrita, and he is so lucky to live in that spot.

Another special thanks goes to Eva and Eleonora whose have read poems in the first hand.. You always have supported me and I will always be grateful to have friends such as you.

I thank my beloved and precious one, in time you will read all this.

And I thank you, yes YOU, who will read this book. Thank you to have dedicate some of your time to this reading.